# A LITTLE EARLY LEARNING POEM BOOK ABOUT THE LETTER C

# A Little Early Learning Poem Book About the Letter C

Walter the Educator

**SILENT KING BOOKS**

# SKB

Copyright © 2024 by Walter the Educator

All rights reserved. No part of this book may be reproduced in any manner whatsoever without written permission except in the case of brief quotations embodied in critical articles and reviews.

First Printing, 2024

Disclaimer
This book is a literary work; poems are not about specific persons, locations, situations, and/or circumstances unless mentioned in a historical context. This book is for entertainment and informational purposes only. The author and publisher offer this information without warranties expressed or implied. No matter the grounds, neither the author nor the publisher will be accountable for any losses, injuries, or other damages caused by the reader's use of this book. The use of this book acknowledges an understanding and acceptance of this disclaimer.

dedicated to all the early learners
across the world

# THE LETTER C

In a cozy cottage by the creek,

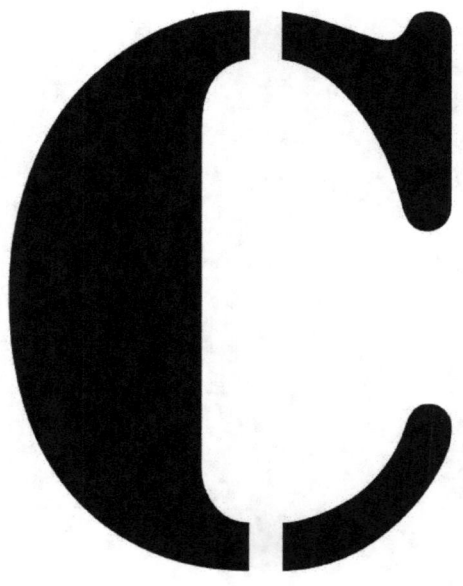

A curious cat named Clementine,

With a colorful coat, so sleek,

Cuddled close by candlelight's shine.

She crafted with care, a tale so sweet,

Of creatures in a land of charm,

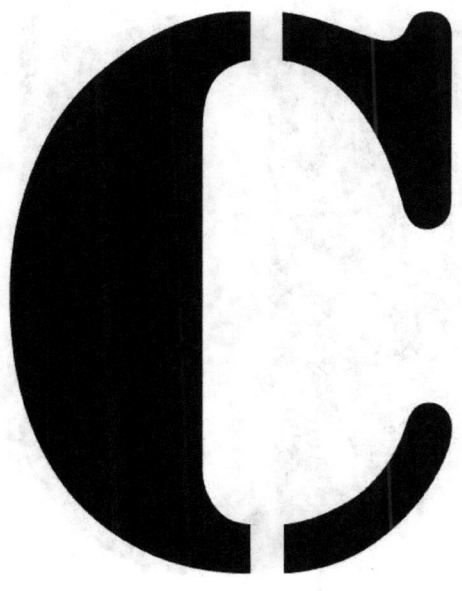

Where the letter C held its seat,

And cast its captivating charm.

"Come close, my dear little ones," she said,

"In a world where castles soar,

And courageous knights with shields of lead,

Seek treasures on a distant shore."

"Let me tell you of a clever crow,

With wings as dark as coal,

Who danced in circles to and fro,

To capture curious souls."

"And in the crystal-clear cascades,

Where clownfish clown around,

They play beneath the coral shades,

With coral castles tightly bound."

"Creatures in the canopy above,

Chirping chorus in the trees,

Their colorful feathers, a testament of love,

As they flutter with the gentle breeze."

"Crickets chirp and crabs scuttle,

Through the sandy coastal cove,

While the cheerful chipmunks hustle,

Collecting nuts with fervent trove."

"In the heart of the enchanted forest,

Lies a cave of wonders untold,

Where the curious bear has made his nest,

In a cozy den to behold."

"Colossal creatures roam the land,

From cuddly kittens to the mighty cougar,

Their claws and teeth so finely planned,

In a world where courage grows ever surer."

"But amidst the chaos and the cheer,

A calliope of colors, vibrant and bright,

A carousel of dreams, drawing near,

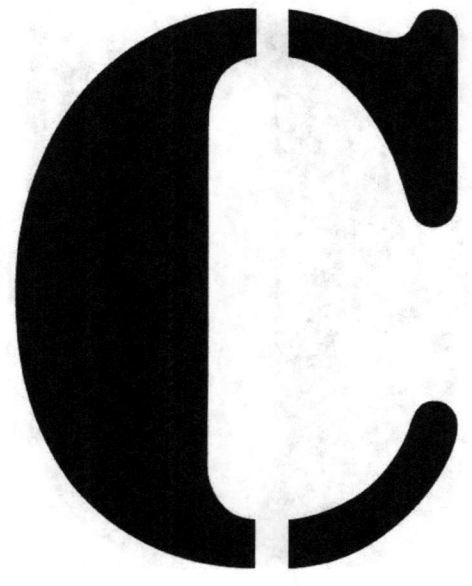

With candy canes and cotton candy, a delight."

"Carousel horses, prancing with glee,

In circles they spin, like a cyclone,

Caterpillars crawl up a cedar tree,

Transforming into butterflies, on their own."

"And in the sky, so calm and clear,

Crescent moon and twinkling stars,

Constellations, a celestial frontier,

Where comets streak like speeding cars."

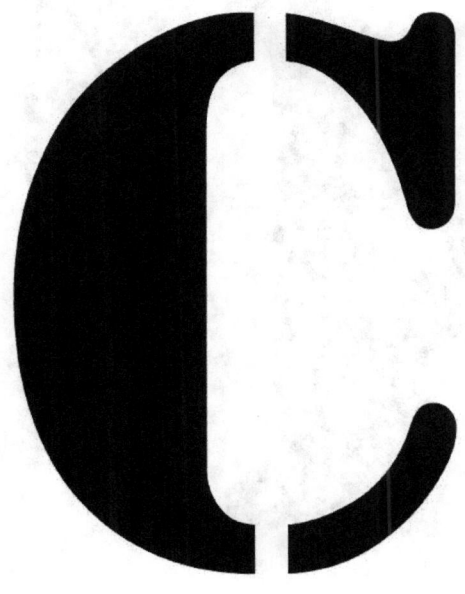

"Children, cherish every cherished moment,

In this captivating world of the letter C,

For in every corner, a curiosity, potent,

A treasure trove for you and me."

So in the cozy cottage by the creek,

The children listened with delight,

To Clementine's tale, so unique,

Under the canopy of the night.

And as they closed their eyes to sleep,

In their minds, the wonders swirled,

In dreams, they ventured deep,

In a world where the letter C unfurled.

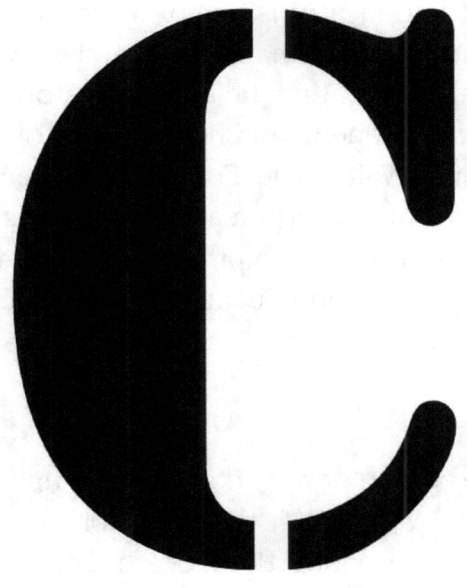

# ABOUT THE CREATOR

Walter the Educator is one of the pseudonyms for Walter Anderson. Formally educated in Chemistry, Business, and Education, he is an educator, an author, a diverse entrepreneur, and he is the son of a disabled war veteran. "Walter the Educator" shares his time between educating and creating. He holds interests and owns several creative projects that entertain, enlighten, enhance, and educate, hoping to inspire and motivate you.

Follow, find new works, and stay up to date with Walter the Educator™
at WaltertheEducator.com

www.ingramcontent.com/pod-product-compliance
Lightning Source LLC
LaVergne TN
LVHW010610070526
838199LV00063BA/5132